Design in fabric and thread

Aileen Murray

Studio Vista

Acknowledgement

My thanks to students at Brighton College of Education, whose work has provided many of the illustrations.

General Editors Janey O'Riordan and Brenda Herbert
© Aileen Murray 1969
Reprinted 1973
Published in London by Studio Vista
35 Red Lion Square, London WC1
Set in 9/9½ pt Univers
Printed in the Netherlands
by Grafische Industrie Haarlem B.V.
ISBN 0 289 79650 4

Contents

Introduction

This book is designed for those who would like to explore the possibilities of creative work with fabric and thread. It is evident in the response to exhibitions and in the work of many schools and evening classes, that there is a growing interest in fabric collage and embroidery.

The term 'fabric pictures' can convey the wrong image, but it is the use of fabrics and threads for framed panels or hangings that I shall consider here. Because there are not the limitations imposed on any embroidery that must stand up to wear, there is more room for experiment. It is not necessary to start with a knowledge of stitches and techniques; your first experiments can be very simple, and you will find that it is easy to learn a stitch when you need it for a particular effect.

Fabric collage is a good starting point, but before long you will realize that it is impossible to hold some fabrics and threads satisfactorily with glue. Then again, you may find that you want to add a greater variety of texture by the use of hand or machine stitching, so that, as the exploration develops, it comes further into the field of embroidery; although the more precise aspects of that craft – details of stitches and techniques – are outside the scope of this book.

The exploration of the nature and properties of the materials makes an excellent starting point. This can lead on to a series of simple experiments, which in turn can be developed into more ambitious designs. This exploratory work will help you to understand the particular qualities of fabric and threads and will therefore enable you to use them more successfully in interpreting a chosen design idea.

1   Materials

Before you start experimenting with design in fabric and threads, it is essential to have a good variety of materials. This need not be very expensive, as small scraps of fabric and odd lengths of thread and wool can be used. It is impossible to make a variety of interesting designs without a wide range of materials. Also, seeing and handling varied pieces of fabric can itself be a source of inspiration and pleasure.

Background fabrics

The choice of the fabric to be used as a background is obviously most important. It must be firm enough to work on without becoming distorted, and just the right colour to help in the development of a particular idea.

Fabrics chosen as a background may be plain, textured, or have some unobtrusive pattern; it is difficult to use a fabric with a strong pattern. Hessian (burlap) is often used, as it makes a good background to varied fabrics. It is available in several widths up to 72 inches and in a wide variety of colours. Many furnishing (upholstery) fabrics are excellent both for their colour and heavier weight; remnant sales may be a useful source of supply for these. Some dress fabrics are suitable, particularly woollens, both plain and tweed; the thinner fabrics are difficult to use as they tend to pucker. A backing of organdie or some other suitable interlining may be used to make a difficult fabric firmer.

Fabrics for making the design

Anyone interested in this work will gradually collect a wide variety of scraps from dressmaking, pieces of furnishing (upholstery) fabrics, oddments of net and lace. It is important to build up a range of textures from thick, rough tweeds to fine, sheer silks, as each type of fabric has its own particular quality to add to a design. A good collection will include fabrics with a nap or pile, those with bouclé or hairy threads, some for their woven or printed pattern, others which are plain but varying from matt to shiny in finish, and a range of sheer, delicate fabrics – chiffons, organza and nets. New materials such as PVC and other plastics are useful, as well as natural leather. Waste materials such as plastic mesh fruit bags and onion bags will give further variety in pattern. Even the common mesh dishcloth or copper pan scourer may be used.

A collection of fabric pieces may be sorted according to colour or kind and stored in polythene (polyethylene) bags so that particular pieces can be easily seen. It is worth keeping even quite small pieces of the more expensive or unusual fabrics.

Fig 1 Fabrics of varied texture

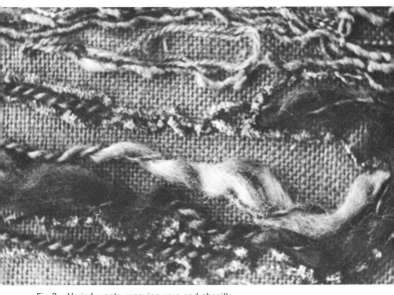

Fig 2 Varied wools, weaving yarn and chenille

Fig 3 Fresca (matt), Perlita (shiny), and thinner soft embroidery threads

Threads

Variety is again important. Embroidery threads of all kinds are an obvious essential, and the thicker ones, such as Fresca (a matt thread) and Perlita (a shiny thread), are particularly useful. All kinds of knitting wool (yarn) and rug wool (yarn) may be available in small quantities. Odd balls of the more unusual and expensive kinds, such as bouclé, mohair, angora, or chenille are sometimes available at a reduced price. Special weaving yarns may have a slub varying the thickness, or some other texture. The threads pulled out from fabrics such as tweeds are another source of this type of textured yarn. String of all kinds, both smooth and hairy, thick and thin, is also useful and so is raffia, both natural and plastic. Decorative cords including gold Lurex cord, may be saved from gifts, together with scraps of ribbon and braid. Pan scourers can be used as a source of copper mesh or wire. Metallic threads of all kinds, from Lurex to real gold, are also available, but some of these are expensive.

Fig 4   Varied strings, some frayed out into fibres

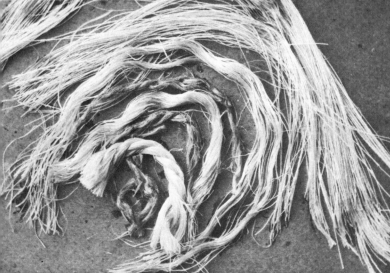

Beads

Beads have been used with embroidery for many hundreds of years to add richness and sparkle. Small packets of dress beads and sequins can be quite expensive, but are worth having. Specialist bead shops have a great variety of kinds and sizes. Handicraft shops usually have at least large china and wooden beads, as well as dress beads and sequins. Cheap or broken necklaces from big stores are another source, particularly for larger beads. Some bead shops sell bags of mixed sweepings which are good value. Small stones, pieces of glass, shells or seeds may all be used in the same way as beads. Larger sequin shapes can be cut from sheets of coloured acetate or bright metallized melinex, a mirror-finished plastic. A varied collection of beads can be stored in small tins (cans) or plastic boxes; the containers used must have tight-fitting lids.

Fig 5   A varied collection, showing small dress beads on lid, assorted large beads and sequins, melon seeds and small acorns

Equipment

Very little special equipment is necessary; a basic list would include:

Scissors medium size for cutting and small for snipping threads.
Needles including very large ones such as chenille needles for heavy threads, crewel needles and fine beading needles.
Adhesive for fabrics flameless rubber solution (U.K.), PVA, Copydex (U.K.), Marvin medium (U.K.), etc., or any flexible white glue such as Sobo or Elmer's glue (U.S.).
A *plastic spreader* or strip of cardboard.
Tailor's chalk or a dustless chalk.
Embroidery frames are often useful.
A *sewing machine* allows a wider range of experiments.

Fig 6   The necessary small items of equipment

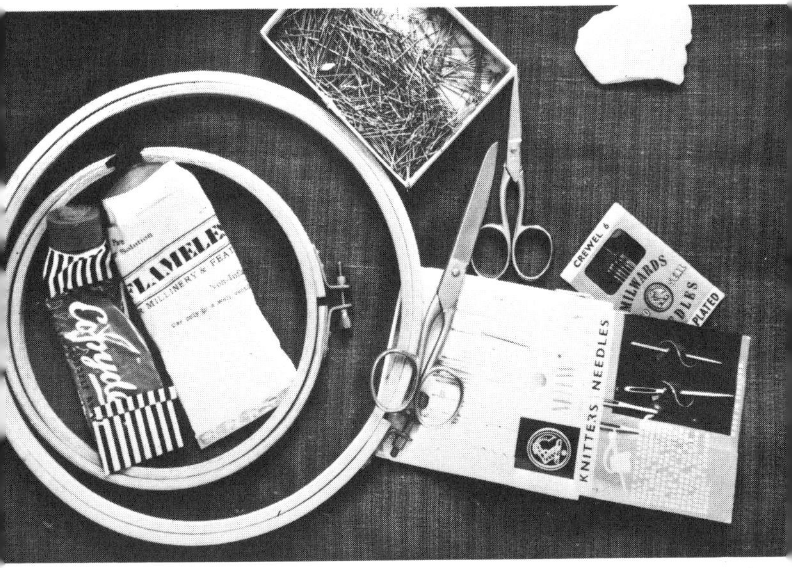

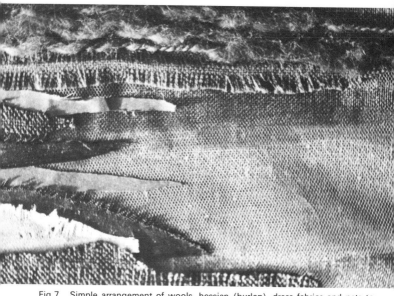

Fig 7 Simple arrangement of wools, hessian (burlap), dress fabrics and nets to show different qualities of texture

Fig 8 Small experiment in texture, including the use of crumpled and pleated chiffons

2 Exploring the materials

Building up fabrics for texture

In building up a successful design of varied fabrics, it is important to make use of the particular quality of each fabric which is chiefly in its texture. It is often a good idea to begin with a design worked in a limited colour range, so that the texture of the fabrics can be fully explored. It is easy to think only of colour; if this is limited you can then begin to consider the effect of the different fabric textures. For instance, the surface quality of white fabrics can vary greatly, depending on whether they are smooth or rough, shiny or dull, fine and semi-transparent or thick, evenly woven or patterned. The quality of whiteness will also depend on the type of fabric; wool is creamy, while cotton may be very white. Light can also affect fabrics, particularly those with a pile and those with a shiny or shot surface. The exact quality of these fabrics will depend on how the light falls on their surface and whether warp or weft threads are vertical. Some shot fabrics can appear quite different in colour when they are turned in different directions. In putting fabrics together all these qualities can be used, perhaps to give emphasis, or to make a slight variation in the background.

Fig 9   Texture from crumpled and frayed fabrics, hessian (burlap), chiffon, nets

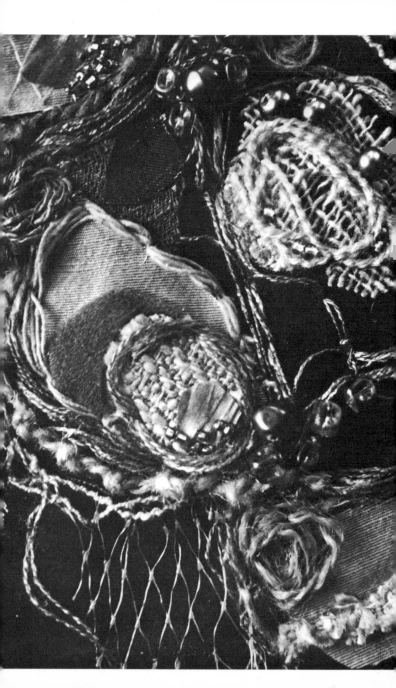

As a first experiment you could make a simple design, perhaps just arranging a group of circular shapes, using one colour only but making use of varied shades and textures. In this way you can learn how to use textures to good effect, as the development of the design will depend on texture rather than colour for interest or emphasis. The exploration of the qualities of fabrics in this way can itself lead to further ideas for design.

Similar experiments might also be made in interpreting the varied surface texture of a piece of bark or stone. You should not try to copy it exactly, but to suggest the shapes, tones and textures seen in it.

Fig 11   Design from repetition of similar shapes with variation in size and texture

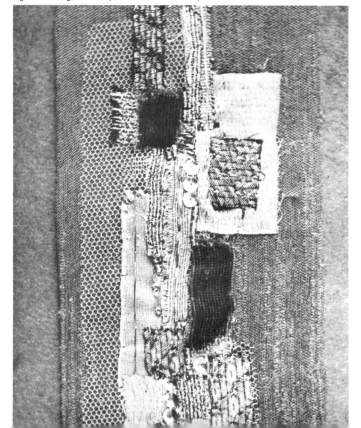

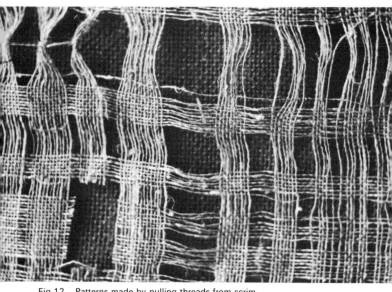

Fig 12   Patterns made by pulling threads from scrim

Fig 13   Scrim distorted by removing threads and pulling the remaining threads apart

Disintegrating fabrics

Another approach is in pulling fabrics apart in order to find further ways in which they may be used. This is only possible with fairly loosely woven fabrics such as hessian (burlap), scrim, some woollens and some furnishing (upholstery) fabrics.

The simplest way to begin is by pulling threads from one edge of the fabric, leaving a fringe, which may be either narrow or wide. A wide fringe can be further developed by knotting the threads into groups in a regular or irregular pattern. A strip of fabric may be fringed on both long sides; if some of the cross threads are pulled out, a new effect is made.

Threads pulled out within the fabric leave ladder-like gaps; again the remaining threads may be grouped together in regular or irregular patterns. Other threads, perhaps with a shiny or rich quality to contrast with the fabric, may be woven in, or a shiny fabric may be placed behind the gaps made. If a very loosely woven fabric such as scrim is used, the threads can also be pulled apart to leave irregular-shaped holes, with the remaining threads in between packed closely together.

The threads pulled out in the process of this experiment will themselves suggest a further type of design. A tangle of thread could be arranged into a shape which suggests the cell structure of a plant and then developed further with stitchery or beads.

Fig 14   Fringe of knotted threads in hessian (burlap)

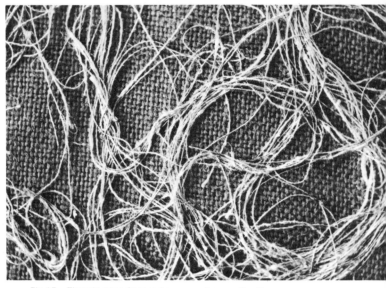

Fig 15   Threads taken from scrim, suggesting a cell pattern

Fig 16   Simple experiment in disintegrated and distorted scrim with the addition of sequins

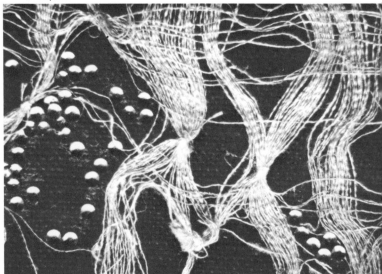

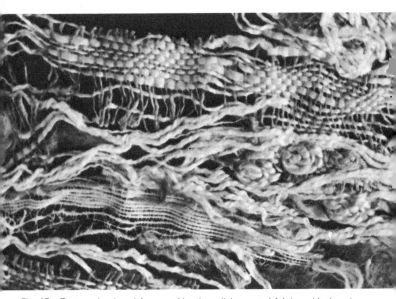

Fig 17   Texture developed from working into disintegrated fabrics with threads and stitchery, detail of fig. 33

Fig 18   Texture from fabric pulled apart with additional stitchery

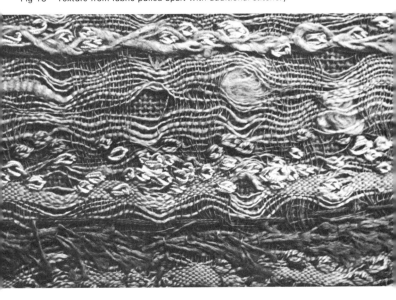

The use of transparent fabrics

Transparent or semi-transparent fabrics provide a particular quality for design, because colours can be mixed or the depth of tone increased by building up several layers of fabric. Coloured nylon dress nets, organza and silk chiffon may be used to build up areas of an intense, glowing colour, either with other fabrics or alone. Subtle intermediate shades can be made by overlapping several coloured nets, or using net over another fabric. Several layers of one colour can be used for the maximum effect; if the size of the pieces is varied, the colour can be made to fade away at the edge. It is fairly easy to achieve a good effect with nets, so one must sometimes be rather strong minded and look for another solution. Too much net over other fabrics can even out the effect, making it rather dull; you may then find it necessary to start cutting some away to reveal the lower layers.

All the experiments mentioned so far would be carried out on an opaque fabric background, but a wide variety of nets, including curtain (drapery) nets and similar fabrics, can also be used to make a transparent design to be seen in silhouette against a light or window. For this, fabrics of varied texture and opacity are glued or stitched onto a firm net background, such as a stiff, square-meshed net.

Fig 20   Plant design using layers of coloured nets with some hessian (burlap)

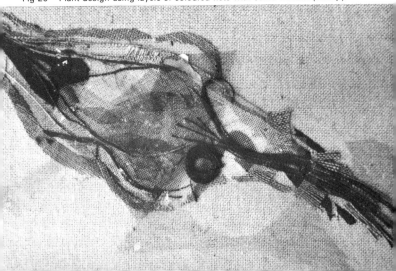

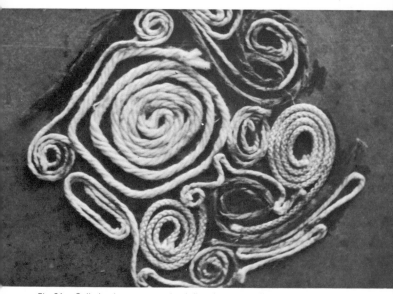

Fig 21   Coiled string patterns glued directly onto cardboard

Fig 22   Experiments in thread lines of varying weight, using stitches over thick yarn, lines of knotted string, thick yarn drawn out into open patterns

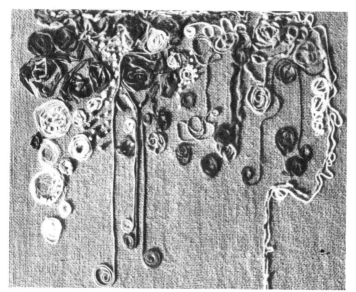

Fig 23 Thread design based on cork texture, partly glued and partly stitched in place (see also fig. 24)

Texture from threads

Threads can give further variety in texture to a fabric design or may be used alone. In either case, a wide range of threads, thick and thin, rough and smooth, are needed to create interest. Certain designs lend themselves to interpretation with threads, for example the flowing lines and knotty textures of a wood grain pattern.

It is more difficult to glue threads than areas of fabric, but it can be done, especially when a shape is filled with a coiled thread pattern. If a whole design is to be made in this way, the thread can be glued directly onto cardboard.

One of the simplest and most effective ways of holding threads onto the background is couching; that is, stitching them in place with a finer thread. If the aim is a free flowing line, a tiny stitch may be made in the thickness of the thread to hold it; on the other hand, the stitching over it could become part of the pattern. It is worth experimenting with ways of breaking the even quality of a line by fluffing out the thread, or knotting it, or working over it with a stitch.

Once stitching is introduced, a much wider variety of knotted and patterned lines and textures becomes possible. It is not at all necessary, at first, to know many stitches, you can begin by experimenting with straight stitches and knots. Later you will be able to build up a repertoire of useful stitches.

Fig 24   Detail of fig. 23 showing the varied threads, raffia and beads

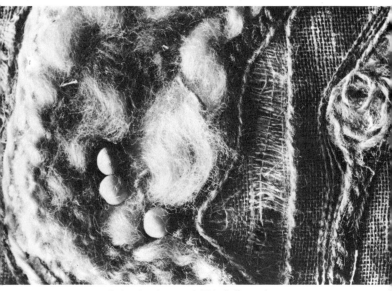

Fig 25   Detail of fig. 48 showing the use of thick, fluffy wool

Fig 26   Detail of fig. 56 showing the use of frayed hessian (burlap) thread with weaving yarn and raffia

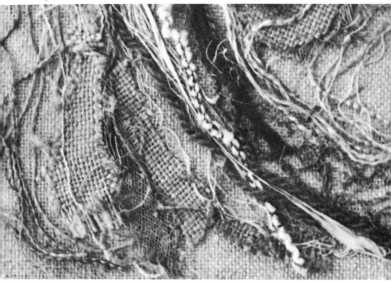

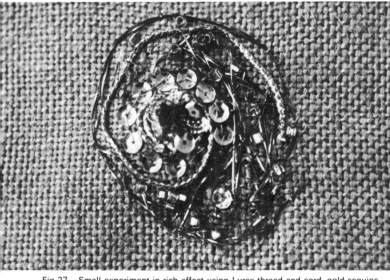

Fig 27 Small experiment in rich effect using Lurex thread and cord, gold sequins and beads

Fig 28 Black richness, a pile up of jet and other black beads and sequins, stitched over a small padded shape. Detail of fig. 47

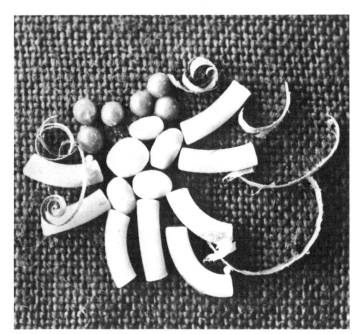

Fig 29 Seeds, pasta and shavings can give a good effect in clusters. These have been glued to the background fabric

Increased richness

A richer effect may be created by the introduction of beads, sequins, or 'jewels' of various kinds and sizes. Thick clusters of beads, emphasizing part of the design, have a more exciting impact than an even sprinkling. You can experiment with ways of grouping beads and ways of attaching them. When using small dress beads, a special fine beading needle is really essential to sew them.

Seeds and shells, although less rich in themselves, may also be combined in rich patterns or clusters. Many buttons are good used in this way; rows of them might fill a whole area.

Large shiny shapes can be cut from gold or silver leather, PVC, thin, bright metal, or coloured acetate. These can be used like outsize sequins and can be combined very successfully with small beads. Gold, silver and Lurex threads, cords and braids can also add richness.

When experimenting in making a very rich effect, it is often a good idea to work on a small scale. Rich and precious things are often small, and a tiny piece of work in various gold materials and beads can have a very exciting impact.

3 Sources of inspiration

Sometimes the idea for a design evolves from a process of experiment with fabrics, but more often it will come from some particular source of inspiration. This is a starting point; you can use it quite directly, or develop the idea and treatment until its source is not easily recognizable. There are many good starting points; different things will appeal to different people, but it is worth being constantly on the lookout for new ideas and experimenting with a wide variety. As your interest develops, you will gradually make a collection of ideas from objects, photographs, sketches and other experiments.

Natural forms

These have been the chief source of inspiration in the past and still provide a rich fund of ideas. Today we may look at these forms in a different way: influenced by science, we look into how things are made and the hidden intricacy of structure revealed by the microscope.

Fig 30   Holes in a chalky stone

Fig 31   A piece of bark worn smooth by the sea

Fig 32   The bark of an old apple tree, encrusted with lichen

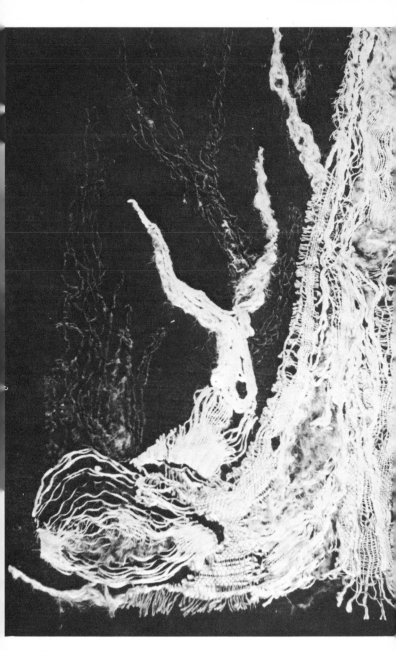

Fig 33 Tree stump design in white fabrics of varied texture, some disintegrated, with some stitchery

Plant forms are a rich source of inspiration. The whole plant is beautiful, but it is often particularly valuable to take a small part of it and to look at it in great detail, perhaps using a magnifying glass. Try doing this with the centre of a flower, the structure of a seed case, or the detailed pattern of a leaf.

Wood patterns lend themselves well to interpretation in fabric and thread. The varied structure of bark, the swirling patterns of grain and wood knots are all worth investigating. Rubbings or prints are often useful to simplify the structure. The pattern of tree trunks and branches against the sky might be another starting point, so too might the twisted forms of roots.

Rock formation, fossils, stones and shells, may all be studied for their beauty of form, or for a detail of pattern or composition. When worn, weathered, or broken by the sea, they change both shape and texture, and may become even more interesting.

Animal forms are another source of inspiration. Birds, fish, insects and reptiles have particularly good pattern qualities in the division of feathers or scales. A study of the bone structure can also be a useful starting point. A natural history museum may be a more valuable place than a zoo to study animal forms, as the details of pattern or structure can be more closely observed.

Fig 34 Detail of fossil shell design (fig. 61) showing varied texture

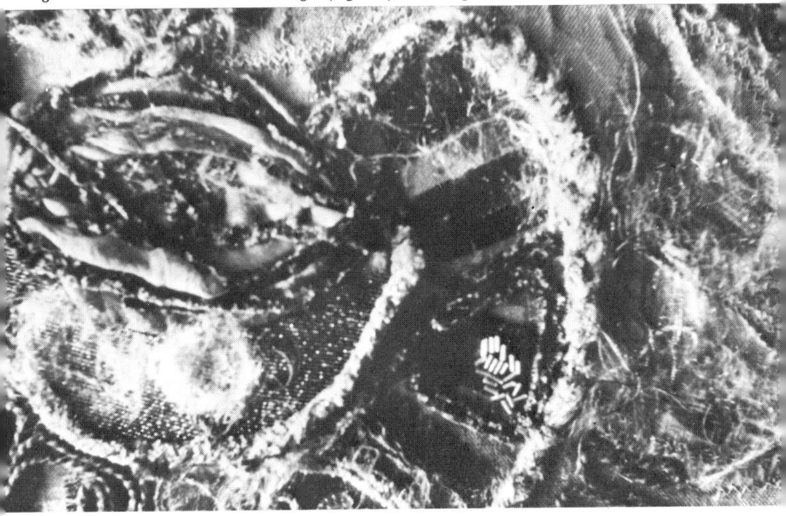

The human figure may also be used, but because of the limitations imposed by working in fabrics, it is easier to find ideas where the figure has been treated very simply, with emphasis on the patterns made by garments. Romanesque and other early forms of sculpture, mediaeval paintings, mosaics, primitive masks and figures, will all prove useful sources.

Man-made structures

These lend themselves to a different sort of treatment. Lines tend to be sharper, shapes more clean cut. Buildings, both old and new, may provide design ideas from their basic structure, or from some detail of construction or ornament. Very often patterns to be found around us in railings, balconies, chimneys, tiles or walls are overlooked unless we stop to observe more closely. The crossing lines of scaffolding, pylons, or the girders under a pier may also become a rich source of ideas.

Machinery of all kinds has a fascination of its own. Moving wheels are often a basic element; these may vary from the large wheels at the pit head of a mine, to the delicate cog wheels inside a watch. Forms of machinery may range from the ancient, simple shapes of some farm implements, to the complicated structure of small parts inside electrical equipment. Some may be studied in a museum, others surround us in daily life if we take the trouble to notice them.

Fig 36   Part of a design based on a treadle wheel, using varied textures in a limited colour range

Ideas could also spring from the way many forms, both natural and man-made, are constructed in units. Many man-made forms are also grouped or stacked together, and pattern can be seen in piles of drainpipes or tiles. This grouping of similar shapes can be developed into most interesting designs.

Simple shapes, such as circles or rectangles, may be cut in various sizes and grouped together. You could also start from the reverse idea of taking a shape such as a circle and cutting it apart in vertical slices, or in wedge-shaped pieces. It is best to try this first on paper, working on a contrasting background. The cut pieces are moved apart without displacing them; several ways of doing this may be tried, allowing more or less background to show, before the design is glued in place.

Further sources

Books may be used to supplement first hand sources, particularly when they give information which would otherwise be difficult to obtain. There are a number of books with excellent photographs of plants, birds, life under the sea, and so on. Some reveal in fine detail the patterns hidden in the structure of a plant, or mineral, or in the forms of minute living creatures. The details of cell structure seen under the microscope is another valuable source of ideas for design.

Photography may be used to collect design ideas, especially if you have the equipment to take detailed close-up views of bark, flowers, stones, and so on. You can then easily keep an idea for future use. Simple slides may be made by putting fragments of leaves, flowers or feathers into a ready-made slide case; when projected, tiny details of pattern are revealed. It is quite easy to change the contents of the slide when desired. Photographs of various interesting forms from natural and man-made sources may also be collected from colour supplements in newspapers and from magazines. It is useful to have some way of keeping these, perhaps grouping similar pictures together in a folder, so that they are easily found when needed.

Looking at varied forms, making sketches, collecting photographs, will make you more aware of the wealth of interesting potential ideas which are so often overlooked. In noticing these things and appreciating their qualities, you may also begin to see how they might be interpreted in fabric and threads.

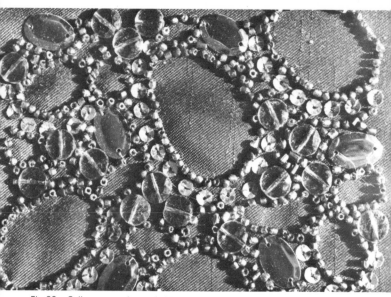

Fig 38   Cell pattern using varied beads and sequins

Fig 39   Cell pattern using copper wire from a pan scourer, with threads and beads

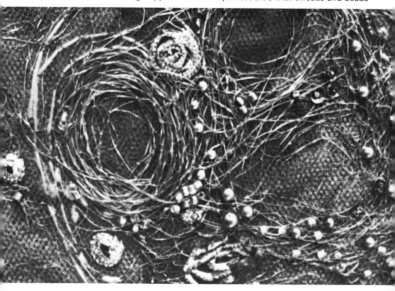

4 Interpreting an idea for fabrics

Having collected a store of materials and found a source of inspiration in an object or picture, you can start working out your design. There are two ways of beginning to interpret an idea in fabrics. One is to work directly from an object or picture, the other is to do some preliminary work on paper first. The first method is often a good one for beginners in this medium; the idea can be worked out very directly, cutting fabrics and experimenting with their arrangement. You can complete the work quickly, before your initial enthusiasm fades, and the result may be very fresh and lively. However, when carrying out a more ambitious piece of work, it is advisable to plan it on paper first.

Planning on paper

This may be done by making a series of sketches investigating a chosen subject, selecting the most interesting parts and making them into a composition. Gouache paints which give a thick, opaque colour are good when working on a design, as they can be used thickly to suggest texture. Coloured inks or tissue paper are useful for flat areas of colour.

As an alternative to painting, you might experiment with some simple form of print making to build up a design. Ideas taken from the shapes of blocks of buildings might be worked out by cutting cardboard and gluing it onto a cardboard block. Then the design is made by printing and over-printing. Dry powder paint mixed with a cellulose paste such as Polycell to a thick consistency can be used for simple prints. Monoprints are a good way to work out ideas from natural forms: the shape is built up by drawing with printing inks or thickened paint on a glass slab, or by thinly coating the slab with ink and rubbing away part of the ink. Prints made in this way are easily interpreted in fabric. You could also experiment in making a design by printing with a potato block, or using scrap materials such as cotton reels and small cartons.

Cut or torn paper may also be used in planning a design. Those who find drawing difficult may be happier working in this way and find the results more successful. It is a good way to design for fabric collage, as it makes one think of the main shapes which will later be cut in fabric.

Various types of paper can be used. Coloured tissue gives a good range of clear colours, which are intensified or mingled by using several layers. Texture can be suggested by using crumpled tissue. Coloured magazine paper allows one to make use of printed textures and patterns in the design. However, one

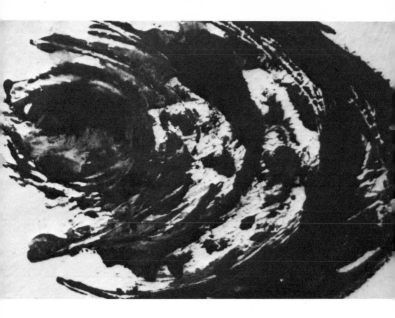

Figs 40 and 41   Monoprints based on plant forms; the varied textures of these prints are easily adapted for fabrics and threads

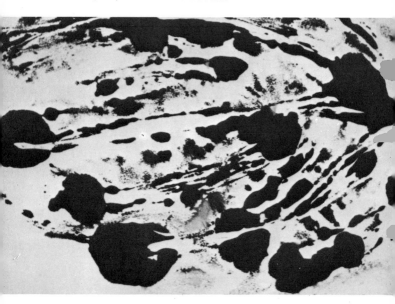

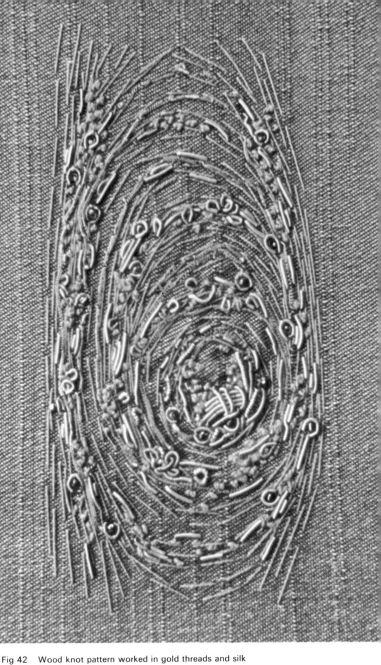

Fig 42 Wood knot pattern worked in gold threads and silk

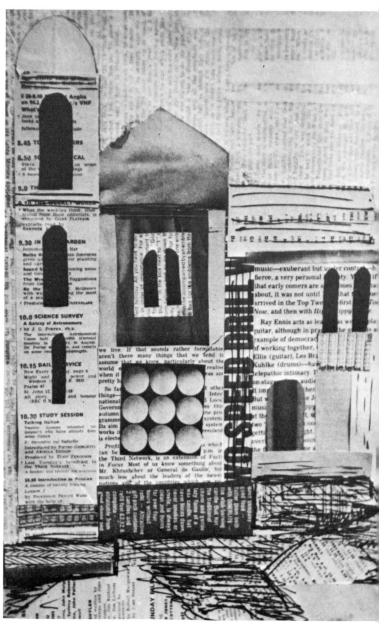

Fig 43 Cut paper design, using tones and patterns from printed paper. See fig. 37 for interpretation in stitchery

Fig 44   Cut paper design using newspaper for varied tones. See fig. 97 for interpretation in fabrics

of the best ways is to use newspaper, simply working in areas of dark, medium and light tone, using the white paper for the light tones, the newsprint for grey, and the illustrations for the darker areas. This is easy to interpret in coloured fabrics of varied tones; and you will avoid the problem of finding that a colour has been chosen which is not available in fabric.

In working out a design in paper, the shapes may be cut to give a sharp-edged effect, or torn to give softer outlines, according to the chosen subject. The shapes cut or torn may be arranged and rearranged several times before they are glued down, and unsatisfactory shapes are easily altered. It is much easier to see the effect of making a change if a shape can just be moved about, instead of being drawn again. Lines of string and clusters of seeds may be added to suggest details, but the design is not yet complete, as it must allow for further development in fabric.

In this planning stage, you must sort out the problems of the arrangement of shapes and lines within a space to give a satisfactory result. In using the cut paper method, it is easier to assess which arrangement is best within the background area and where the main centre of interest should be. Some people have a natural feeling for this, others learn slowly by experimenting and by looking at successful designs to see how they are made.

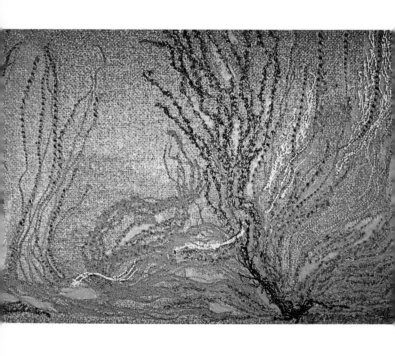

Fig 45   Adaptation from landscape, with varied threads, many pulled from a tweed
fabric

Colour and tone

Other problems to be considered relate to colour, tone and texture and though these can be worked out on paper, it should be done with reference to the materials which will be used. You should therefore work with your chosen range of fabrics close at hand.

It is perhaps easier, at first, to work out an idea in a closely related scheme of colours, such as yellowish greens ranging to blues, or golds to browns. You may then feel the need to add a touch of a strongly contrasting colour. It is often surprising how a small touch of an unexpected colour can bring a whole design to life. Each person tends to find a favourite range of colours, but it is good to experiment more widely. Observation of the range of colour present in one form, such as a flower, may be helpful to those who find the choice of colour difficult. You should also notice how a colour is changed by various backgrounds and by the amount of it used in a design. The same red will look different on a light background and on a dark one and will have a different effect when used in large or small amounts. Light will affect colours too, so, when working in artificial light, it is best not to go too far before checking the colours in daylight.

Tone is also very important; there must be a satisfactory balance between dark, medium and light toned areas. It is necessary to be particularly careful with the placing of very light areas of fabric that will catch the eye, considering how they are placed within the whole area. An uneven arrangement of tones is generally more interesting than one which is very evenly balanced. In selecting colours, their tone value must therefore be taken into account.

Texture can be used to alter colours and tones. By adding areas of stitchery, thread, or net, it is possible to catch the light or make a subtle change of colour. Here again it is the effect of light on varied surfaces which is important.

Adaptation for fabrics

Whatever the source of inspiration, the idea must be adapted in terms of the materials used. Fabric pictures which copy the treatment of paintings, or in which similar fabrics are used as areas of flat colour, are less successful than those which make use of the particular quality of fabrics, especially their texture. This will include the use of frayed edges and the drawn thread techniques which break or distort the fabric surface.

Fig 46   Eastern building, showing a treatment which is flat and yet richly patterned

A design idea must allow for the way in which it can be treated in fabrics. When representing a building, animal, flower or figure, realistic effects are not very suitable. It is better to look at the lines and shapes, patterns and textures within the form, which may become simplified and flat in treatment. Although it may be unsatisfactory to aim at a three-dimensional or realistic treatment, it is quite possible to use some raised or padded areas, simply to enrich or emphasize part of the design.

You must consider whether a design should be simply treated in large shapes, or broken down into the richer detail of small shapes within larger ones. Thread lines may be used in many ways, to make an outline, or to develop textures or patterns within shapes. The whole design must be integrated to avoid becoming a collection of unrelated parts. Areas of background fabric are as important a part of the design as any of the applied fabrics, so their shape and size in relation to the other fabrics should be carefully considered.

Fig 47   Cell structure worked in black fabrics and beads, showing the great variation in tone and surface quality found in one colour

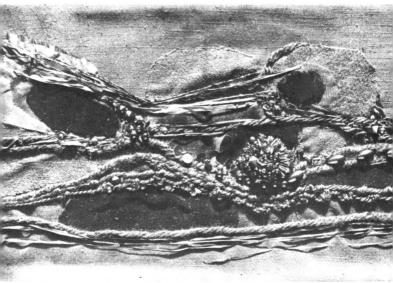

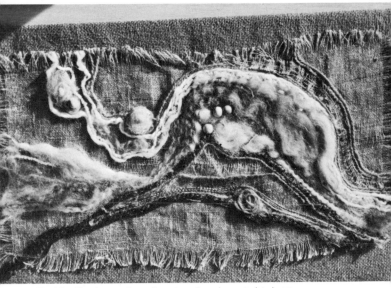

Fig 48   Simple experiment in texture, based on a twisted root

Fig 49   Fabrics and threads of varied texture in a more carefully controlled design. Detail of fig. 99

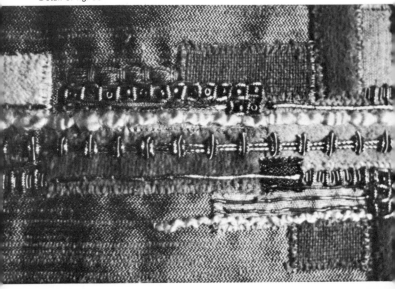

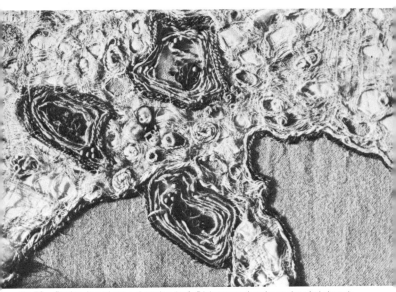

Fig 50   Design based on a decaying leaf. Disintegrated scrim and varied threads
emphasize the worn, textured surface

Fig 51   Detail of fig. 50 showing the use of threads in open areas

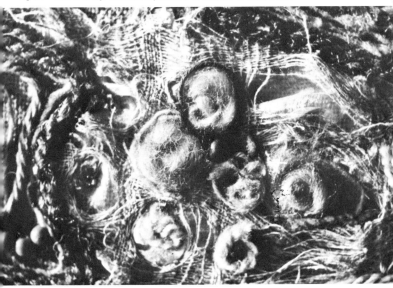

49

5   Working out a design in fabrics

Ways of beginning

With either a design on paper, or something to work from and an idea of how to interpret it, you are ready to begin. The background fabric should be large enough to allow for mounting. It is a good idea to leave a fairly generous border, two or three inches at least. This makes mounting easier and also allows a little room for the design to spread out in working. The background fabric should be cut on the straight grain and any creases pressed out. If the fabric has an uneven weave, consider carefully before cutting which way of the fabric should be vertical to give the best effect.

Some people begin straight away by cutting and placing the main shapes on the background, others like to have a few guiding lines. Tailor's chalk, or any dustless chalk, can be used to draw the main lines or shapes and it will rub away without marking the fabric.

Another simple method, for a more precise design, is to make a tracing of the main outlines, pin this over the background fabric and tack (baste) around the lines with fairly small stitches, taking care to fasten the ends of the thread firmly. The tracing is then torn away and the tacked outline is left on the fabric. These simple methods are sufficient for this type of freely adapted work.

Sort out the scraps of fabric to be used and press any that are crumpled. Make sure that there is an adequate range of threads in the colour scheme you have chosen, checking if threads drawn out from any of the fabrics will be suitable.

Building up the design

There are several ways of building up a design from pieces of fabric. You can start with large shapes and work over these with smaller shapes and details, or the whole design can be made up of quite small pieces. In some cases a particular shape may be used; for example, in a bird design, pieces may be cut to suggest the shape of feathers. Large, precise shapes are best cut on the straight grain of the fabric; but with smaller pieces in a freely worked design, it is often better to cut them so that the grain works in with the lines of the design. Fabric edges need not necessarily be neatly cut, fraying may add the right textural quality.

It is important not to be too eager to fix the pieces into place, as one of the advantages of this work is that pieces can be moved or adjusted slightly to improve the general balance of the design. Once the main parts are in place, pin them securely and have a good look at the work from a distance. If possible pin (tack) it up on a wall or, if this cannot be done, put it on the floor and look down on it. It is easier to see if the general effect and balance of the design is right when looking at it from some distance. It is then possible to make any alterations that seem necessary, and it often helps to do this while the work is up on the wall. If you are doubtful about what to do, or whether a change is needed, it is often wise to leave the work for a while. Coming back to it after an interval of time, you may find it easier to see what changes are needed.

Fig 52   The start of a design; only the background layer is in position

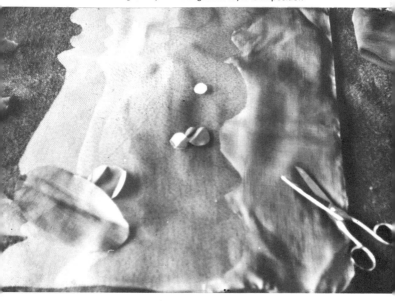

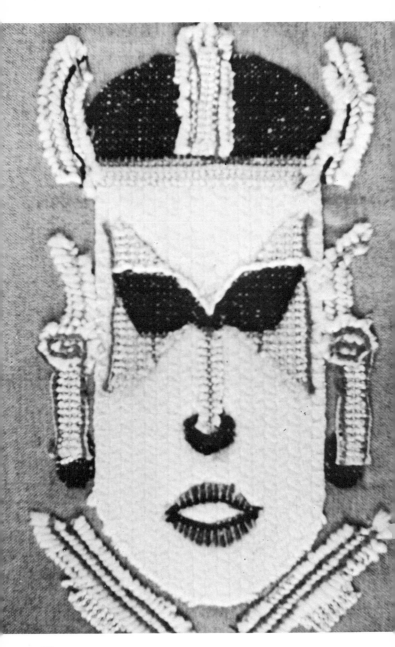

52

Methods of fixing down the design

The main shapes are generally fixed in place before smaller details are added. This can be done by gluing, or stitching by hand or machine. Gluing is obviously the quickest method and is suitable for all fabrics except those that are very delicate and thin. A lightweight rubber solution prepared for the millinery trade is one of the cheapest satisfactory adhesives; it dries quite quickly and does not mark the fabric, the only disadvantage is its strong smell. There are other rubber and PVA adhesives which are quite suitable for this purpose, but more expensive. It is necessary to use enough adhesive to hold the fabric, particularly at the edges, but too much may mark the fabric and will make it very stiff. This makes it more difficult to add any stitchery at a later stage. As gluing is such a quick method of working, it is particularly good for first experiments in this medium, as results can be achieved quickly before enthusiasm wanes.

Fig 54   Wood grain design quickly glued in place; this could be further developed with machine stitching or embroidery

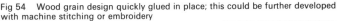

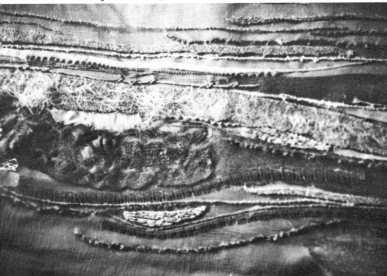

Fig 55   Design in rectangles of varied fabrics and gold PVC, partly glued and partly stitched in place. Some parts are slightly padded

Hand sewing is the second method for fixing the design in place. It is much more suitable than gluing for delicate fabrics. When nets or chiffons are used, they can be held in position with a running stitch which is very tiny on the right side but is widely spaced out, with an inch or more between stitches on a simple shape. Heavier materials can be held in place with small, straight catch stitches which will hold the piece almost invisibly. Another alternative to both these methods, where the line of the edge is to be more clearly defined, is to use a suitable decorative stitch. As this type of work does not have to stand up to wear, it is not necessary to neaten each edge firmly with stitching. Lines of stitchery or couched thread should only be used to outline an edge where this is required by the design idea. Other edges may be left undefined by way of contrast. Hand sewing is suitable for all types of fabric. It will give a very secure finish, but is obviously slower than gluing.

Fig 56   Wood grain pattern mainly held in place by hand sewing; it is difficult to glue these fine thread lines. See fig. 26 for detail

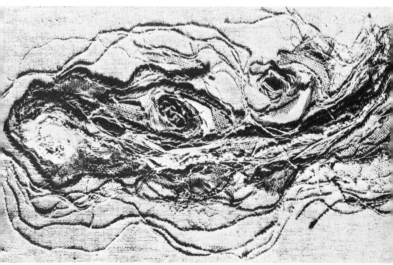

If a sewing machine is available, this will give a quicker result. The pieces may be held in place with a line of machine stitching along the edge, or with part of a machine texture which covers a wider area. In the first case, the line could be of straight or zig-zag stitching; an open zig-zag is frequently used. When machine stitching over fabric pieces, it is better to tack (baste) them in place first, although it is possible to machine stitch simple shapes that are only pinned in place, provided that the pins are at right angles to the line of stitching. It is obviously necessary to take care that the fabric pieces are quite flat and do not move under the machine foot. Machine stitching is a quick and very secure method of attaching fabrics or threads and is the obvious one to use if machine-stitched textures are to form part of the design, (see chapter 6). It is suitable for any type or weight of fabric.

Fig 57   Flower design in nets and chiffons held with machine stitched lines and textures

Fig 58   Small cellular pattern enriched with Lurex threads, cord and varied beads

Completing the design

When the main shapes have been fixed in place, further small fabric shapes and thread lines or textures may be added. These can be fixed in place by gluing or sewing as before. Great care is needed when developing the design in this way, so that each small part adds something to the whole. It is only too easy to become carried away in one's enthusiasm to enrich the design, with the result that it may become over-elaborate or unbalanced. It is important to look at the work from a distance from time to time to judge the total effect. The development at this stage may include the use of machine-stitched textures, hand stitchery or beads. You can experiment with simply placing threads and beads in position in order to decide where – or whether – they should be used.

When to stop is a very important decision, which may be quite difficult to make. You must decide when the design has reached a state of balance; although this does not mean an even treatment of all areas, but rather, an interesting arrangement within the background space. Whether to stop at once, or to do a lot more work on all parts of the design, may depend on whether the general effect required is one of richness or simplicity. Again, it is often helpful to leave the work for a while and then to look at it afresh after an interval.

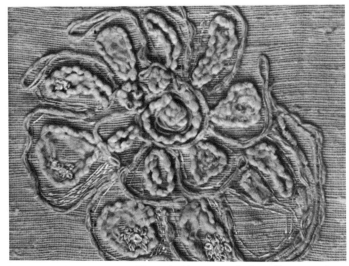

Fig 59   Fossil shell pattern in machine embroidery on net; the heavy lines are made with a thicker thread on the bobbin (spool)

Fig 60   Fossil shell pattern in white threads of varied texture

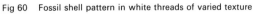

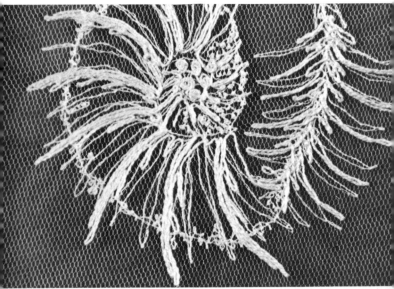

Variety of effect

It is fascinating to see a group of people working on a similar theme, interpreting their ideas in their own choice of fabrics. Although the starting point was similar, the results may be quite different according to the way in which the idea has been envisaged and developed in fabrics and threads. Similarly, one person can experiment in working on a chosen theme in a variety of ways and, because the choice of materials must to some extent dictate the way in which they are used, each version will be very different. Many artists have become obsessed by a theme in this way, trying out not only a variety of materials and techniques, but different ways of expressing the essential idea which has caught their imagination (see figs 59–61).

Fig 61   Fossil shell pattern in fabrics and threads, with variation of colour and texture to give a rich effect

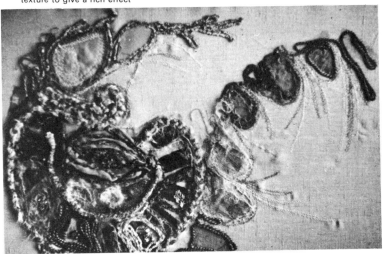

6   Machine embroidery

Choice of machine

Any domestic sewing machine, even the simplest and oldest, can be used to sew pieces of fabric in place and to add simple lines and textures. Obviously the newer machines have many advantages, such as a swing needle for zig-zag stitching. They also have a very easy adjustment to lower the teeth, or feed, for free stitching. It is possible, however, to use an older machine for this free stitching embroidery as long as it is an electric model, as both hands are needed to control the work.

One great advantage, when using a machine for embroidery, is the ability to switch easily from straight to zig-zag stitch, or to alter the stitch length or spacing, while the machine is moving. On some machines it is very easy to do this, while on others (even some good and expensive machines) it is more difficult. If you are buying a new machine this is an important point to consider. The set 'embroidery' patterns produced by a fully automatic machine are not very useful in this type of work, as they are more difficult to combine into a successful design; so a fully automatic machine is not worth the extra expense unless you have another use for these patterned stitches, for example on children's clothes. On the other hand, a machine which has a slow speed gear is very good for free embroidery. Although the better machines are expensive, there are now some good swing-needle machines in the cheaper price range. When choosing a new machine, it is usually a question of finding the best value within a set price range. It is always wise to try out the machine to find out whether it is easy and convenient to use.

It is important to know your machine, how it works and what it will do. Instructions about threading and the purpose of the various controls cannot be given here, as different makes of machine vary. The best thing to do is to study the book of instructions supplied with your machine and to make a series of simple experiments, altering the size or spacing of the stitch. It is an interesting exercise to find out how many types of lines and linear textures can be made simply by machine stitching up and down a piece of fabric.

It is also an advantage to know a sewing machine well enough to make simple adjustments and to keep it clean, oiled and in good order. The more complicated adjustments needed when something goes wrong should be left to an expert.

Fig 62   Assyrian figure in varied fabrics applied by machine stitching, with a machine-textured background

Machine stitching to attach fabrics

Any type of machine may be used simply to attach fabric pieces onto a background. In making a decorative fabric panel, there is not the same concern for a hard-wearing finish that there would be for a household article. Fabric pieces may therefore be machine stitched in place with a straight or zig-zag stitch on, or near, the edge of the shape. Probably the best choice is an open zig-zag stitch, if this is available. It is better to tack (baste) the pieces in place first, but it is possible, with care, to machine stitch pinned fabrics, if the design is not very exact. Pins should be placed at right angles to the line of stitching to avoid breaking machine needles. If fabrics are not tacked (basted), it is important that they should be quite flat before working across them.

It is wise to work right across the fabric, machine stitching the pieces down before adding further lines or textures. Great care is needed when machine stitching circular shapes to avoid puckering the fabric. Machine embroidery is easier on a firm, closely woven background, but a backing such as organdie may be used with a more loosely woven fabric, to prevent stretching.

Invisible nylon thread may be used if it is desirable that the line of stitching should show as little as possible. Generally, any machine thread in a suitable colour can be used. Some firms make a special machine embroidery cotton, which is finer than the ordinary cotton and better if the machine stitching is to be developed in a thick texture. The size of needle used will depend on the type, thickness and layers of fabric which are to be used.

Machine stitching is one of the best ways of attaching delicate and transparent fabrics such as net, chiffon and thin nylon. Further lines or textures which may be developed will also show up to best advantage on these materials.

When planning a design with fabrics and machine embroidery, the whole design can be built up before machining, or the first layer can be machine stitched in place before adding smaller details. In either case it is possible to add further pieces at a later stage, if necessary.

Thick threads and wools can also be held by machine stitching. A zig-zag stitch can be used over the thread, either closely spaced so that the thread is covered, or widely spaced so that it shows through. It is also possible to fix threads less exactly by using zig-zag stitching into one side of them, or holding them with a wandering line of straight stitching.

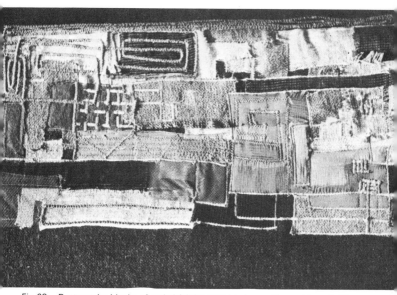

Fig 63   Rectangular blocks of varied fabrics held in place with machine stitching and enriched with further line patterns

Fig 64   Detail of fig. 63 showing bars of machined satin stitch and heavy threads held with a zig-zag stitch

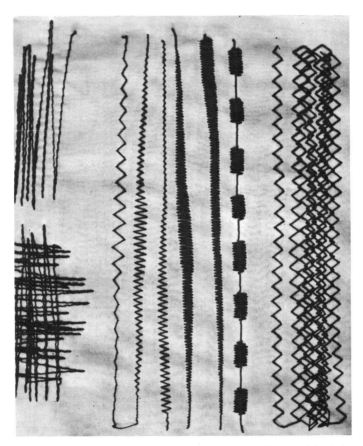

Fig 65 Simple textures made by machine stitching to and fro in straight stitch, then variations in zig-zag

Simple line patterns and textures

Many line patterns and textures may be developed by simply using the machine in the normal way and experimenting with various stitch settings. Obviously more variety is possible with a swing needle machine.

By machine stitching up and down the fabric with straight stitching, using the reverse button or lever (on an old machine the work must be turned each time), you can make heavier lines, or work over an area with a grass-like texture. Solid areas of stitching can be built up by working to and fro over a small area of fabric, or textures can be made with crossing lines.

With a swing needle machine you can experiment with the width and spacing of the stitch, which will cause the weight and quality of the line to vary. Broken lines can be made by switching from straight to zig-zag stitch while working. Here it is helpful to have a machine which allows this change of stitch to be made easily without stopping. If it is necessary to stop the machine, always make sure that the needle is up before altering the stitch, otherwise the needle becomes bent and will break. Richer textures may develop from the use of a number of lines of zig-zag stitch massed or grouped together. Still further variations are possible by altering the spacing of the stitch used or by working another series of lines across the first.

It is possible to work quite a variety of simple textures in this way, using the normal machine foot. The limitation is that they must all be worked to and fro across the fabric. Any curved lines must be worked with great care to avoid puckering the fabric. These textures may also be combined with the use of thicker threads applied with machine stitching (see page 62).

Fig 66   Simple textures in zig-zag stitch combined with drawn thread and woven bands of raffia

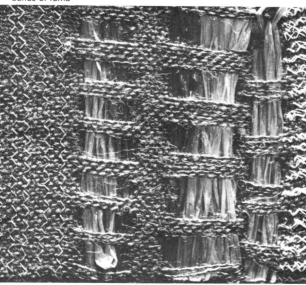

Free stitching for machine embroidery

ADJUSTING THE MACHINE

Most new machines can easily be set for free stitching, which makes it possible to work a much wider and richer variety of textures. The way to set the machine is usually described under the heading of machine darning in the instruction book. The teeth, or feed, which moves the fabric, must be lowered by pressing a button or turning a lever; in some cases this raises the plate over the teeth. On older machines, a raised, screw-on plate may be available to serve the same purpose. After this adjustment, with the teeth out of action, the fabric can be moved quite freely in any direction. Many machines provide a special light foot for darning and embroidery, so that the fabric can be controlled yet freely moved; otherwise it is necessary to remove the foot. Because there is only a light foot or none at all, the fabric must be tightly stretched under the needle, so when working without a foot, or on thin fabrics, a ring frame should be used (fig. 67). If you are using the light foot on heavier fabrics, it is possible to hold them taut between the hands.

BEGINNING TO WORK

To stretch fabric in a ring frame, place it over the larger, outer hoop, right side uppermost; then put the smaller hoop on top, tighten the screw, and pull the fabric taut. In this way the fabric will lie right side up and flat on the machine base. It is important that the fabric should be tightly stretched in the frame.

When starting a piece of machine embroidery, both ends of thread should be brought through to the right side of the work and held together behind the needle. The presser bar must be lowered even if you are working without a foot, or there will be no tension on the top thread. Several stitches are then worked on the same spot to fasten the thread, and after moving away the ends of thread can be cut. As the teeth no longer control the movement of the fabric, the size of stitch will depend on the speed at which it is moved. For a small stitch, machine fast and move the frame slowly; for a long stitch, machine at a moderate speed while moving the frame quickly. The length of stitch you use will depend on the quality of line you want to make.

You can hold the frame in whichever way you find comfortable; generally the hands should be placed evenly on each side, keeping the fingers back from the needle. It is necessary to learn control of the machine to work it smoothly, and also to move the frame or fabric at an even speed under the needle; jerky movements tend to break the cotton. It takes some hours of practice to gain real control, especially when working slowly. Some sewing machines have a slow speed gear which is useful both when learning and for intricate work.

Fig 67   A machine prepared for free stitching, showing the light darning foot and the fabric stretched in a ring frame

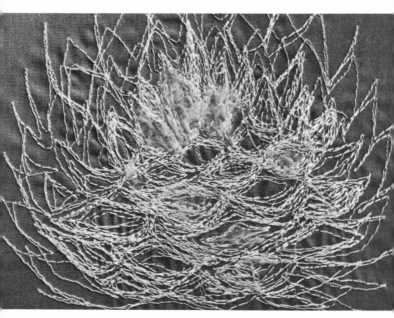

Figs 68 and 69 Textures based on cacti, worked in free stitching with some applied fluffy thread

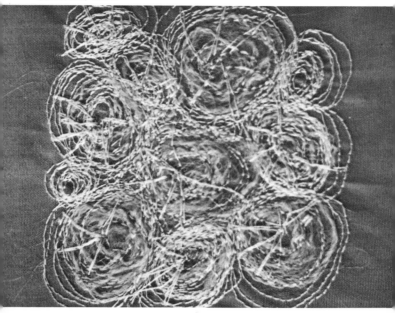

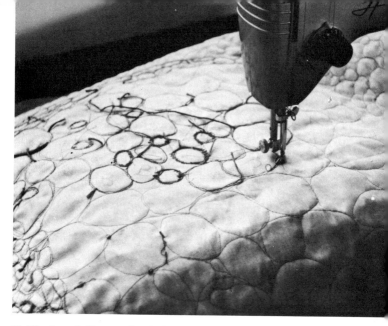

Fig 70   Free stitching on a heavier fabric, working without a frame. This texture, with heavy thread on the bobbin (spool), is being worked on the wrong side. (See page 73 and fig. 75.)

Textures from free stitching

Textures may be made with a simple line to and fro as before, but, with the feed lowered, it is possible to move the fabric freely in any direction, including circles and curving lines. Many useful textures may be based on circular shapes; these can be developed as pebble textures made of solid or open shapes, or a 'scribble' texture of curling lines, known as seeding. Other shapes such as rectangles or triangles could be used in a similar way. Textures of this sort may be made with both straight and zig-zag stitching; the latter is distorted in an interesting way by moving the fabric freely. Probably you will first just experiment to find out what can be done; there are endless possibilities, depending on the size and type of stitch and the direction of movement. Later, texture ideas may be based on specific forms: the bark of a tree, the leaves of a cactus, or the pattern of a stone wall.

The sewing machine may also be used to draw forms such as shells or flower centres. This can be quite fascinating as an experiment, but you should take care to make use of the particular effects and textures of machine stitching and not just copy a drawing.

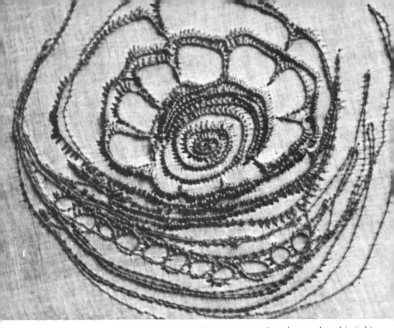

Fig 71   Machine texture experiment using uneven tension; the top thread is tight and the bobbin (spool) tension loose

Fig 72 (*opposite*)   Cell structure design in varied fabrics with some machine textures

Free machine stitching may be combined with the use of a thicker thread which can be attached with a zig-zag stitch to give a corded effect. The thick thread can be pinned in position before stitching. A heavy corded line is made if a close zig-zag is used, but a widely spaced stitch will give a softer effect. The thick thread may also be attached more freely with a random straight stitch line. Take care that the foot does not catch in thick thread or wool.

A further range of experiments can be made by using an uneven tension. If the lower tension is loosened, this thread will come up in small loops around the upper thread. This is best done with a fine machine embroidery thread on the bobbin (spool) and a slightly heavier upper thread, such as an ordinary sewing cotton. If the machine is worked quickly while the fabric is moved slowly, a raised, whipped line is formed. If the fabric is moved more quickly the stitch has larger, more uneven loops. This type of stitch looks well when worked in circular or curving patterns. Although some effects are more conventionally correct, what really matters in experiments of this kind is whether the effect obtained is the right one for the purpose.

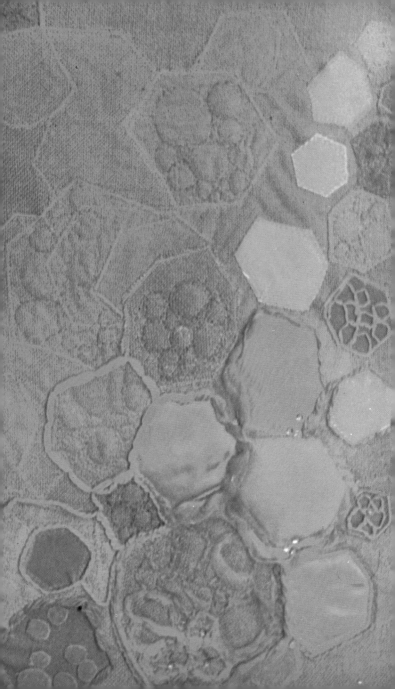

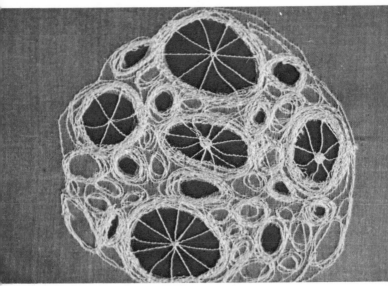

Fig 73   Machine stitching on delicate fabrics: organdie with cut work patterns

Fig 74   Machine stitching on delicate fabrics: on net with applied spots of organdie

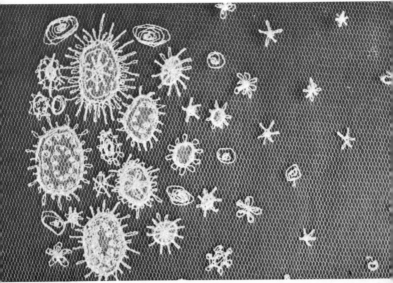

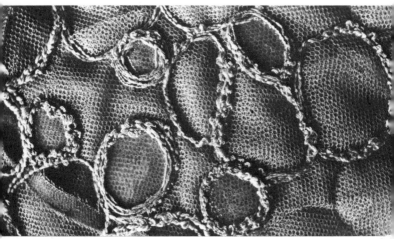

Fig 75   Cell structure worked on the wrong side with soft embroidery cotton (thread) on the bobbin (spool)

All these methods are fairly simple and can be used quite freely after a little practice. You can also experiment in the use of various materials, especially delicate fabrics such as chiffons, nets, organdie, when interesting effects can be made by over-lapping two or more layers. Machine textures may be made on organdie with applied nets, or on net with applied areas of organdie. To apply spots of fabric, it is easier to work on a double layer of fabrics, outlining the shapes with machining and cutting away the surplus fabric of one layer. Machine textures can also be combined successfully with heavier fabrics, although the effect would be different.

There are other, more complicated techniques used in machine embroidery, which require more practice. One is to use a thicker thread on the bobbin, for which a looser lower tension is necessary; by working on the wrong side of the fabric, attractive heavy lines are made on the right side (see above and fig. 70). Another technique is the use of machine stitching to outline shapes, which are then cut away inside the lines of stitching; if two layers of fabric are used, a contrasting fabric may show through the holes (see page 89).

When using machine embroidery on a large piece of work, the design must be constantly considered as a whole. It is easy, especially when working in a frame, to concentrate on one part, which may result in an unbalanced design.

This chapter can only be an introduction to machine embroidery. Further reading and experiment will open up new possibilities to anyone interested in this aspect of work with fabrics.

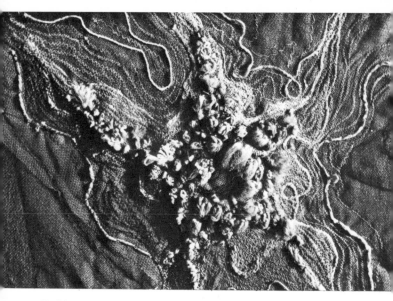

Fig 76   Jellyfish design with applied nets, machine textures and knot stitches in varied threads and wools

Fig 77   Simple experiment based on a ridged stone, using straight stitches in varied threads

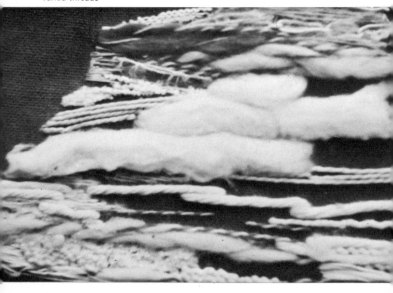

7 Further development

Experiments with stitches

You will not go very far in experimenting with fabric and threads before wanting to introduce some hand stitches for a richer and more varied effect. It seems logical to progress from experiments in fabric collage to a need for additional embroidery, and then to learn or invent the stitches which will give the desired effect. There are a number of useful books giving details of stitches and how to work them (see page 101). Those which group stitches of a kind are easy to use and it is good to have photographs as well as diagrams. However, books are only a starting point for individual experiment.

   Much interest and variety comes from the use of different types and weights of thread. The same stitch will look quite different worked in a fine silk and in a thick wool. The simplest use of straight line stitches can be made interesting in this way. Very thick wools can make a simple stitch look more impressive. A special heavy embroidery needle, sometimes called a chenille needle or knitter's needle, is necessary for these thicker threads.

Fig 78   Detail of stitchery, including lines and solid areas

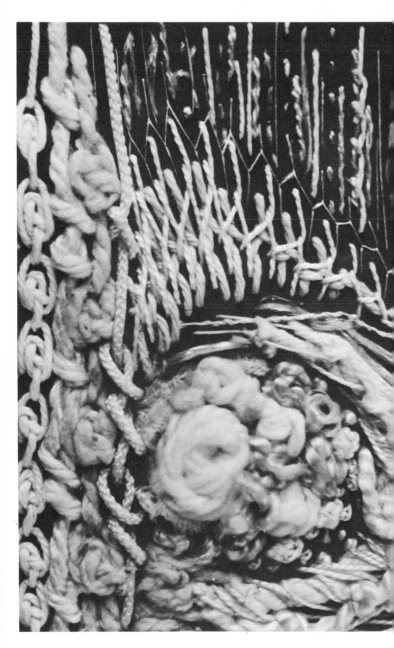

Fig 79   Small experiment in stitchery, using flat and knotted stitches in varied
threads

As you experiment with embroidery you will gradually build up
a repertoire of favourite stitches. There are, for instance, a variety
of knotted stitches, but you will probably use only a few of them
and each individual's choice will vary. Often the simpler stitches
are more useful and more adaptable. In this type of embroidery,
there is no virtue in even, regular stitches; a line which is uneven
in size or irregular in spacing may be more effective.

It is well worth experimenting with hand stitches alone. This is
best done on a fairly small scale as it is obviously a slower method.
Routine samplers have little value, but to fill a small shape with
a pattern of stitches, perhaps limited in type or colour, is a useful
and demanding experiment. For example, a small area may be
covered with line stitches or knotted stitches, varying the thread,
direction of stitch and spacing to create the maximum interest. A
flower centre or wood knot pattern could be the starting point for
a similar experiment, this time trying to interpret the lines and
textures of the chosen form.

Fig 80   Small experiment based on a flower centre, including eyelet holes, knotted
and line stitches

Fig 81 Detail of canvas work in fig. 37, showing the varied use of stitches, with flat and looped strips of fabric

Experiments can be made in the use of colour with stitchery. The same stitch texture might be worked on a self-coloured background, making a subtle variation in texture, or on a contrasting colour when it would stand out strongly. When a contrasting fabric is used as background, the spacing of the stitches and amount of fabric showing through them becomes very important. Some stitches, especially straight ones such as satin stitch, are strongly affected by changes of direction which may alter the colour tone.

Further variation may be made by an unusual choice of thread and background, for example by using thick threads on a delicate

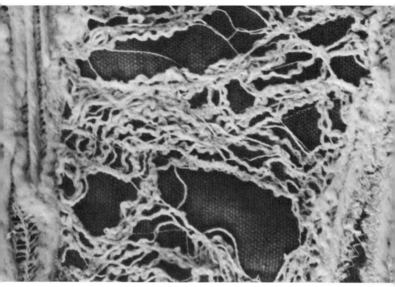

Fig 82 Experiment in drawn thread, the remaining threads grouped by machine and some use of stitchery

fabric. Similarly, stitchery of different kinds may be successfully combined; for example, eyelet holes with chunky knots in a heavy thread or wool.

Although it is not necessary to know a great many stitches at first, since many can be evolved through experiment, those who already have a knowledge of stitches and techniques can make use of it. Some traditional methods may be used in a new way, taking the essential idea and altering the size or spacing of the stitches, or the type of materials used. Variations made on drawn thread techniques are particularly interesting. Contrasting shiny threads or beads can be combined successfully with drawn thread; so, too, can the use of machine stitchery. Experiment may also lead to the use of stitchery on a different scale. For example, canvas work can appear in quite a new light if varied threads, types of stitch and even strips of fabric are used on a coarse canvas sold for rugmaking.

After experimenting, many people will probably choose to make use of stitchery to enrich fabric collage, rather than entirely on its own. There is still plenty of scope for using stitches in a variety of ways; they may add lines or specific details of pattern, or add a rich texture, or be used to alter the appearance of an area of fabric in some subtle way.

Fig 83   Weaving experiment on a simple cardboard loom

Fig 84   Detail of another weaving experiment with varied materials

The use of woven threads

Further knowledge of the qualities and textures of fabrics and threads can be gained by combining them in woven patterns. These may first be treated as small experiments, but could be developed into decorative hangings.

No special equipment is necessary for this type of weaving. The simplest type of 'loom' is made by cutting slits or notches evenly spaced along two opposite sides of a piece of firm cardboard. A strong thread or string is then wound between the slits, to and fro over one side of the cardboard. It should be quite taut but not tight enough to bend the card. It is wise to begin and end the pattern with a band of regular weaving in a firm thread or wool. This should be darned in with a thick needle or bodkin (blunt needle).

After the firm beginning, you can include a variety of threads, wools, raffia, or strips of fabric woven in regular or irregular patterns. Variety of texture is made by the method of weaving; that is, the number of threads passed over before going under one. The thread you are working with may be woven right across a complete row, or can be turned back part way across to build up a smaller block or wedge shape. Other materials such as thin pliable twigs, strips of bark, feathers, dried leaves, grasses or seed cases may also be worked into the woven patterns. The cardboard is removed when the work is finished.

Fig 85   Pattern of weaving and stitchery stretched in a frame

A circular woven pattern may be made, using a large copper wire lampshade ring for the outer circle and a curtain ring for the inner one. Thread or string is tied between the two, first making the four quarters so that they are held in place, and then filling the spaces in between. Again a variety of threads and strips of fabric are used to work around in circles or part circles, starting from the centre ring. Beads might be added by stringing them onto some of the threads. The working framework for this type of weaving is also its frame and so it is not removed when the work is complete.

Another type of partly woven, partly stitched design is worked in a rectangular wooden framework. Threads are stretched across this frame, either from small tacks, or from holes made in the frame sides. Or you can fix folded strips of fabric with small tacks or staples to cover the frame, with the neat, folded edge towards the inner space; threads are then stretched across in both directions by stitching through the folded edges, either with regular spacing or in irregular groups. A firm, strong thread should be used for this purpose. A variety of threads are then used to build up a design within this framework, using stitches such as herringbone and blanket-stitch together with woven patterns. Threads can be bunched together, further lines including diagonals and heavily worked areas can be added. This type of design is

Fig 86   Detail of fig. 85 showing worked areas and interest from varied texture in a limited colour range

generally best if worked in one colour; interest is developed by the weight of thread and stitchery used. Again, the working structure is also the frame for display; usually a suitable fabric backing is fixed in place. The finished work needs careful lighting, as shadow patterns cast from the threads can add interest.

Woven patterns made with varied threads, ribbons or strips of fabric may also be used to alter or enrich the appearance of fabric. They can either be worked into loosely woven furnishing fabrics, or into fabrics from which bands of thread have been drawn. This method of working can be quite simple, but interesting effects are possible by working bright colours into a neutral background, or by contrasting rich and shiny materials with a dull textured one. The methods used may include the traditional ones associated with drawn thread and needle weaving, or you can experiment freely with haphazard groupings of threads. Interest may also develop from the contrast between solid and open areas, especially where these are not evenly balanced.

Woven techniques could become part of a fabric collage, either by applying woven areas or by working in this way across a hole in the background fabric. Mixing methods in an unexpected way can be very successful, but it must be done with due regard to the total effect and balance of the design.

Fig 87   A circular pattern produced by the tie and dye method by pleating from the centre

Fig 88   Band patterns produced by the tie and dye method from horizontal pleating

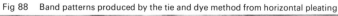

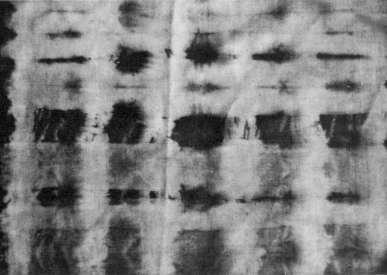

Dyed or printed background fabrics

An alternative to using a ready-made fabric background, is to dye or print it yourself. This might be useful if a particular colour or texture proved very hard to find. If a pattern or texture is merely required as a background for collage or embroidery, the simpler methods of patterning are best. What is required is a basis on which to work, not a fully developed design.

Tie and dye is one of the most suitable methods to combine with embroidery. It is also convenient, as it is easy to carry out at home using Dylon dyes (cold water dyes, such as Tintex or Rit, in the U.S.) which are quite cheap and easy to obtain. The fabrics used must not be too firm and heavy or they cannot be tightly tied. Machine embroidery, which is successful on thinner fabrics, is one of the best methods to combine with dyed patterns.

The piece of fabric to be dyed can be pleated and folded across into a very narrow strip and then tied tightly with narrow or wide bands of thread or string, spaced at intervals along it. The covering of string resists the dye and produces a pattern arranged in stripes or bands. A circular pattern can be made by twisting or pleating the fabric from a central point with all the edges together, then tying it as before. Spot patterns are made by knotting the fabric at regular intervals, or tying it tightly around a small stone. These · are some of the simplest methods of tying; there are many others described in full detail in a book on this subject (see page 101).

It is necessary to follow accurately the instructions given with the dye, and to rinse thoroughly to remove loose dye; and it is better to allow the fabric to dry before undoing the string. A further colour and pattern may be added, either by increasing the width of the bands of string, or by undoing the ties and fixing the fabric into a new pattern. It is usually more successful to start with paler colours, and then add the darker ones. The string will also become dyed and is worth saving with other threads for future use.

Circular patterns may be further developed or enriched with lines or textures in machine embroidery. The centre could be filled with a thick texture of stitchery, perhaps introducing some thicker threads and beads, or lines could be extended outwards from the shape. Further shapes of fabric or net could be applied to fit in with the dyed pattern. Band patterns in muted colours might be used as a textured background on which to build up a fabric collage. If the background fabric is a little light to take the weight of applied areas, it could be used with a firmer interlining. Pieces of tie-dyed fabrics could also be applied in a fabric collage.

Fig 89   Machine embroidery, with applied threads and plastic mesh, on a rather uneven tie-dyed pattern

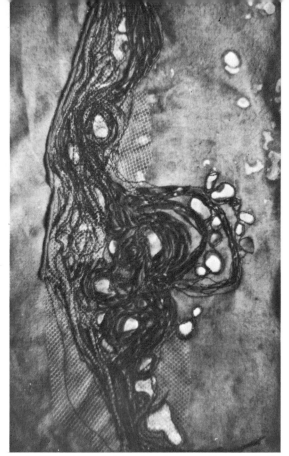

Fig 90   Machine embroidery, with applied threads and nets, working over a batik spot texture

Anyone with the necessary knowledge and suitable equipment could also experiment with other methods. Batik, in which wax is used to resist the dye, can produce patterns and textures which will combine well with embroidery. Simple printed shapes could also be used; more complicated designs are less suitable, as they do not leave room for further development.

The development of dyed or printed patterns with fabrics, threads and stitchery is limited by the shapes of the pattern. Any additions must fit into it, enriching some areas, while making others less conspicuous. This type of work is less free in some respects than work on a plain background; however, if successfully developed the dyed or printed pattern can give a sense of unity to the design.

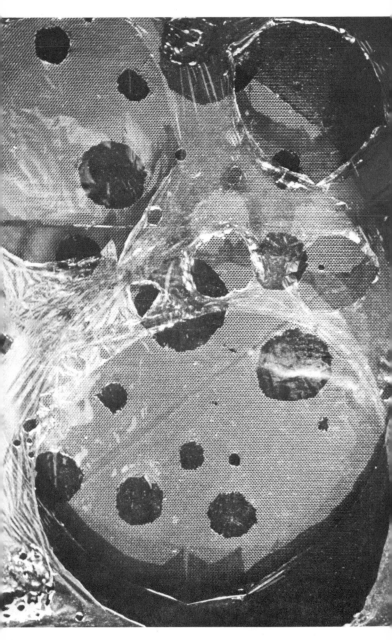

The use of several levels of fabric

A further development, which seems to be of particular interest at the present, is the use of more than one level of background fabric. The usual practice is to have a piece of fabric with a design including one or more holes in it, and behind this, a lower layer seen through the holes. Many variations can be made on this basic idea. Obviously this is a more complicated method and there is more to go wrong, so it is better to have some experience in fabric collage and embroidery before trying it.

The design idea you choose must be one which will lend itself to this treatment. Generally one made of simple shapes is best. The design treatment must be carefully worked out so that both levels and any stitchery or fabrics used are properly integrated. The fabric for the upper level should be firmly woven so that it does not become distorted when cut.

The whole design is built up, areas of fabric are applied, and any machine textures worked. The shapes to be cut should be firmly outlined with machine stitching; a close satin stitch will give a firm edge, or a number of lines of straight stitching, making a

Fig 92   Part of a small design worked on net with machine embroidery; areas cut away reveal clusters of beads on the lower level

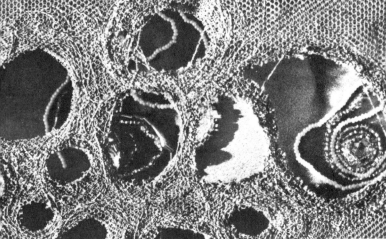

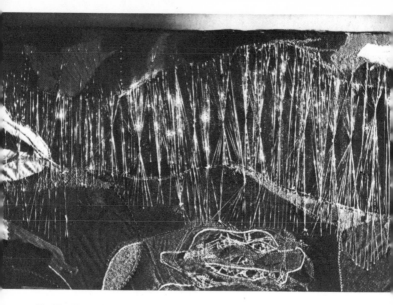

Fig 93 Varied fabrics with machine texture make a background to a large open area covered with patterns of Lurex thread. This idea was based on a cave with stalactites

firm band, could be used. The larger the hole, the stronger the edge should be. Any further work, such as hand stitchery or beading, is then completed. It is best to stretch the fabric by tacking or stapling it over a wooden frame before the holes are cut, otherwise the stretching will be difficult. If the holes are large, it may be neces- sary to work bars of thread across them to keep them in shape.

Another way of making a large circular hole is to mark the shape with chalk and, after completing any applied areas or embroidery, to cut out the hole a little inside the marked line. A circle of firm wire is then made to the correct size and put in place. The edges of the circular hole are snipped, turned back over the wire, and held in place with a line of running stitches. This gives a fairly firm edge, so that any stitchery can be completed and the work stretched quite easily.

The upper level of fabric could include open areas of pattern, partly stitched, partly woven, as described on pages 81–83. Where smaller holes are used, cobweb patterns in machine stitching may be worked across the empty spaces (see fig. 73).

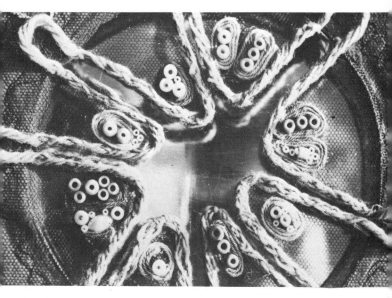

Fig 94   Circular hole stiffened with wire around the edge; wire also supports the heavy thread pattern. The threads and beads are reflected in the bright metal below

There are a number of ways of treating the lower layer of fabric, which is usually fixed across the back of the wooden frame. The depth of frame will vary according to its size and the particular effect required by the design. The upper level may be simply treated and the lower, seen through the holes, very rich with glistening beads. Contrasts or progressions of colour may be used, perhaps with a darker shade below to increase the sense of depth. Another idea is to use a very bright, shiny surface such as PVC, metallic foil, bright reflecting metal, or metallized melinex, a sheet plastic coated with a mirror surface. This last idea can be especially interesting, as reflected images will become part of the design.

This method can be further developed, using more than two levels of fabric, but elaboration does not necessarily give additional interest. Great care must be taken in working out the design, to make sure that both parts are so well related that they will be seen as one. The depth of frame between layers needs to be considered, as this can alter the effect. Finally, the use of special lighting can be made to create shadows or emphasize glitter.

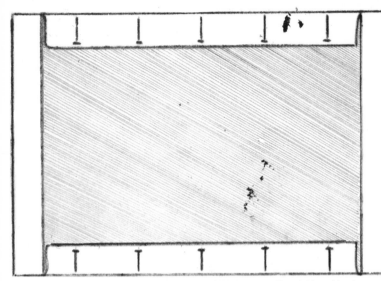

Fig 95   Diagram to show the mounting of fabric on cardboard. Two sides have been pinned back over the cardboard and the corners have been cut away

Fig 96   Hessian (burlap) mounted on cardboard, showing the position of pins and the finish of a corner

8 Simple methods of mounting or finishing

Preparation of the fabric

When the collage or embroidery is finished, the background fabric may have become slightly crumpled or distorted. Any pressing should be done on the wrong side over a soft pad. It is easy to press the edges but more difficult to deal with areas where layers of fabric have been applied, particularly when heavily beaded.

The best way to deal with crumpled or distorted work is to pin (thumb tack) it out on a board which has been covered with a few layers of damp, absorbent paper such as newsprint or blotting paper. Great care and a good deal of time must be given to pinning out the fabric so that it is straight and smooth. It is best to start in the centre of one side and work outwards, and then to do the opposite side in the same way; then repeat with the other two sides. If the fabric is left pinned in position until the damp paper is quite dry, it should be straight and flat when removed.

Mounting on cardboard or hardboard

This is one of the simplest ways of making a rigid finish. The cardboard used should have a hard, compact surface and be rigid enough so that it will not bend. Grey millboard is very suitable and so is hardboard; softer cardboards may become affected by damp weather. Sometimes a thicker board gives a better finish, and for this softboard (softwood) could be used.

The traditional way of holding the fabric in place is by lacing with firm thread or cord. This is a very efficient but rather slow method. Place the cardboard in position on the reverse of the fabric, leaving enough fabric all round to turn over. Then lace the cord across the back from top to bottom, through the turned-over edges of the fabric, pulling the fabric tight. Repeat the lacing from side to side; these cords may be laced between the ones running from top to bottom. The fabric should be tightly stretched; small adjustments can be made by pulling up or easing out the cord. Corners should be trimmed or mitred for a flat finish.

An easier method is to glue the edges of the fabric onto the back of the cardboard. The amount of fabric turned over to the back should not be greater than about one inch or it will be difficult to keep it flat while gluing. Place the cardboard in position on the reverse of the work as before. It is a good idea to pin the edges of the fabric in position, putting in the pins at a sharply slanting angle to hold down the fabric. Start from the centre of one side and work outwards to the corners; then repeat with the opposite side. In this way you can check whether the design is correctly placed before gluing. Copydex (Sobo) is one of the best adhesives for this purpose. Again, work opposite sides in pairs, and when gluing the second one of a pair, pull the fabric so that it is tightly stretched. A simple way to finish the corners is to trim away a rectangle of fabric to avoid bulk (see figs 95 and 96). When turning over the remaining flap, bring it back at a slight angle from the edge to prevent it showing on the right side. The reverse side may be neatened by covering it with a piece of strong paper which has been cut just a little smaller than the cardboard so that it will not show on the right side when glued in place. On thicker board it is also possible to attach the fabric with staples.

If the piece of work is to be hung up, a wooden batten (thin wood strip) will be needed to take the screw eyes. Place this in position on the back, and mark around the edge, and then cut away the backing paper from the marked area so that a firm join can be made. The batten (thin wood strip) can be fixed in place with a contact adhesive such as Evo-stik or Elmer's glue.

Fig 97   A quick fabric collage, mounted on cardboard and framed

The use of a fabric covered mount

Some pieces, particularly smaller ones, may be enhanced if put onto a larger mount, which generally looks best covered in fabric. The work is mounted as before and the size of the larger mount is decided. This is covered in exactly the same way with fabric which is usually chosen to match one of the colours used in the design. The position of the mounted design is then marked on the larger mount with a chalk line, and the fabric in this central area is then cut away to within one inch of the marked line so that cardboard can be stuck to cardboard for a stronger finish. Use a contact adhesive such as Evo-stik or Elmer's glue to fix the design in place, and fix a batten (thin wood strip) on the back as before.

Stretching fabric over a wooden frame

Another way of stretching a fabric design is by fixing it onto a wooden frame. This is particularly good if the finished work is to be framed, as it is easier to fix the outer frame to the thickness of the stretcher frame. The stretcher frame is first prepared and assembled; one inch square lengths of wood are suitable for most work. The corners can be mitred and strengthened with a triangle of hardboard, or an interlocking joint can be made by cutting each end to half thickness. The fabric is best held in place with staples from a staple gun or with small tacks. As before, fix the top and bottom first, then the sides, starting at the centre of each edge and working outwards, and pulling the fabric tight as you work. Care must be taken to ensure a neat finish at the corners.

Mounting woven fabrics

Small experiments in woven texture can be tacked (basted) onto a suitable fabric backing. The ends of the weaving can form a decorative fringe which will lie on the fabric. This is then stretched over a piece of cardboard as described already.

An alternative method is to use a window mount (mat). Cut a window shape the required size from stiff cardboard, leaving a suitable edge for the mount. For the best effect, cover this with fabric, stretching it over the cardboard and gluing it to the back round the outer edge. Then cut away the central area of fabric a little inside the window, snip the corners, and turn under and glue the inside edges. The woven pattern can then be secured in the frame, either by gluing at the back, or by sewing the threads cut from the loom in place at the back of the mount (mat). Any raw edges at the back can be covered by gluing on a frame of paper or thin cardboard.

Woven designs may also be finished as hangings by fixing the upper threads from the loom to a wooden bar. The lower ends of thread can be knotted into a fringe if allowance has been made for this.

Framing

A simple frame may enhance the work and give a better finish, though a more elaborate frame is generally less suitable. A simple flat strip of wood or aluminium which fits onto the edge of the wooden stretching frame is often used, or sometimes a frame which projects slightly is effective. The present trend is not to cover fabrics with glass, although sometimes glass is used for very delicate work. The texture and quality of the fabric is much more evident if it is left uncovered, as glass reflects the light.

Fabrics mounted on cardboard may be fixed in specially made frames which have a little ledge inside to take the mounted work; this is similar to framing any picture. Alternatively, wooden battens (thin strips) can be fixed along each edge of the cardboard with Evo-stik or Elmer's glue, and a flat framing fixed to this.

Fabric mounted on a wooden framework is easy to frame with a simple flat wooden framing which can be tacked or glued in place. Other forms of framing such as aluminium or plastic strip may also be used.

Fabric hangings

Another method of finishing is to make a fabric hanging; this is most suitable for a long, narrow shape. The fabric hangs from a wooden bar or dowel, and another is generally used to weight the lower edge so that it will hang still.

A stiff interlining of Vilene (Pellon) or canvas is necessary in most cases so that the work will hang straight. This is cut to size, and the side edges of the fabric are turned over it and held in place with glue or herringbone stitch. A thin fabric lining may be added for a good finish, with the sides turned under and slip-hemmed into place.

Fig 98   Design based on machinery, stretched on a wooden frame with a narrow framing strip

There are several ways of finishing the ends. The simplest is to turn a hem at each end and machine stitch in place, then insert a wooden bar or dowel into the hems. The lower edge may be fringed if the fabric is suitable and a wooden bar can then be put

Fig. 99 Cross design in applied fabrics, gold and beads, finished as a hanging

into a facing strip machine stitched above the fringe. Another way
is to secure both ends of the fabric between a pair of wooden
strips, tacked or glued together. In each case the work is hung
from the upper bar.

It is essential that everything is very securely fixed in place
on a fabric hanging, because of the possible movement; machine
embroidery is therefore more suitable than fabric collage. There
are perhaps more problems in designing a successful fabric
hanging than in designing a rigid panel, but it is a method of
finish which is particularly suited to the nature of fabrics.

Keeping fabric collage or embroidery clean

This is normally not too great a problem, unless there are many
raised areas of fabric to catch the dust. The simplest way to
remove a little dust is to shake it out by tapping the back of the
work. Another method is to use a suitable light attachment on the
vacuum cleaner and to move it gently to and fro, an inch or two
away from the fabric. This will draw out all the dust.

With reasonable care, there is no reason why fabric collages or
embroideries should not last for a very long time. There are
examples of embroidered hangings and upholstery that have
lasted for three hundred years. Of course, work which is stitched
by hand or machine should have a longer life than that which
is glued. An expert dry-cleaning establishment might be
able to deal with an embroidery which had become soiled but
would not be able to clean a fabric collage as the cleaning solvents
would affect the adhesive.

Another risk is that moths may attack the fabrics, particularly
if a woollen fabric is used for the background. Fairly frequent
moving and shaking will chase away moths as well as dust. A
more certain solution is to use the spray type of moth-proofer
designed for use on clothes; this should protect the fabrics
without harming them in any way.

It will be clear from this chapter that, having finished a piece of
collage or embroidery, you must then spend a good deal of time
and effort in finishing and mounting (matting) or framing it.
Professional framing is expensive, so it is worth mastering this
yourself. *Picture Framing for Beginners* by Prudence Nuttall,
in the same series as this book, is a helpful guide to the subject.
Any effort is well worth while, as the choice of mount or frame
and the standard of finish can greatly enhance the final appearance
of a piece of work.

Postscript

This book may prove a useful introduction to work with fabric and threads, as a good deal of ground has been covered in a short space. The books suggested for further reading give both possible sources of ideas and more detailed information on some methods.

Beware of directly copying someone else's work. You can study it for an idea of how to use the materials, but it is better to find your own source of inspiration from an object, sketch, or photograph and to work from that. The interpretation will then be your own, even if you have used the fabrics in a way that is very similar. It is best to start simply and to progress to more complicated methods of working as you gain confidence and experience. The ideas and methods suggested here have been arranged in this way.

A further useful source of ideas is to visit exhibitions of fabric collage or embroidery and to make a first-hand study of the materials and methods used. There are now a number of exhibitions which visit various centres throughout the country.

Fig 100

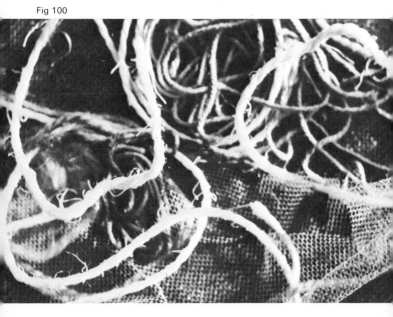

Further reading

Books on work with fabric and threads

Inspiration for Embroidery by C. Howard; Batsford, London and Branford, Newton Centre, Mass.

Machine Embroidery by J. Gray; Batsford, London

Simple Stitches by A. Butler; Batsford, London

Embroidery Stitches by B. Snook; Batsford, London

Design in Embroidery by K. Whyte; Batsford, London

Designing with String by M. Seyd; Batsford, London and Watson-Guptill, New York

Decorative Wall Hangings by D. Van Dommelen; Nicholas Vane, London and Funk and Wagnalls, New York

Colour and Texture in Creative Textile Craft by R. Hartung; Batsford, London

Tie and Dye as a Present Day Craft by A. Maile; Mills and Boon, London and Taplinger, New York

Introducing Batik by E. Samuel; Batsford, London and Watson-Guptill, New York

Weaving is for Anyone by J. Wilson; Studio Vista, London and Reinhold, New York

Books for design ideas

Nature as Designer: a Botanical Art Study by B. Bager; Warne, London and Reinhold, New York

Plant Marvels in Miniature by C. Postma; Harrap, London

Forms and Patterns in Nature by Wolf Strache; Studio Vista, London and Pantheon, New York

Life in the Sea by L. Nilsson and G. Jagersten; G. T. Foulis, London

Life under the Microscope by O. Jirovec; Spring Books, London

Living Invertebrates of the World by R. Buchsbaum and L. J. Milne; Hamish Hamilton, London

Snow Crystals by W. A. Bentley and W. J. Humphreys; Dover, New York

Structure in Art and Science by G. Kepes; Studio Vista, London and Braziller, New York

The Education of Vision by G. Kepes; Studio Vista, London and Braziller, New York

Primitive Art by D. Fraser; Thames and Hudson, London and Doubleday, New York

Larousse Encyclopedia of Byzantine and Medieval Art by R. Hughe; Hamlyn, London and Putnam, New York

Suppliers (Great Britain)

FABRICS
Boyle's Muraweave hessian (display weight) and furnishing fabrics from furnishing fabric shops and department stores.
Dress fabrics, nets, etc. from dress fabric shops and department stores.
Scrim, usually sold for window cleaning, with household linens.

EMBROIDERY THREADS AND OTHER MATERIALS
Dryad Ltd, Nothgates, Leicester, LE1 4QR.
The Needlewoman, Regent Street, London W1.
Nottingham Handcraft Co., Melton Road, West Bridgford, Nottingham.
Specialist shops in many towns and some large stores.

BRAIDS, FRINGES, METAL THREADS, CORDS AND SILKS
Louis Grosse Ltd, 36 Manchester Street, London W1.

METAL THREADS
Toye, Kenning and Spencer Ltd, Regalia House, Red Lion Square, London WC1.

BEADS
Ellis and Farrier Ltd, 5 Princes Street, Hanover Square, London W1.
Sesame Ventures, Greenham Hall, Wellington, Somerset (postal orders).
Some stores and embroidery shops.

GOLD AND SILVER KID
The Light Leather Co., Soho Square, London W1.

PLASTIC FABRICS
B & G (Leathercloth) Ltd, 147 Cleveland Street, London W1.

ROPE, STRING AND CANVAS
Mister Bosun's Locker, East Street, Chichester.
Russell and Chapple, Monmouth Street, London WC2.

COLOURED ACETATE
Rank Strand Electric Co., 29 King Street, London WC2.

METALLIZED MELINEX OR LUMALINE
Aluminium Coatings, Faraday Road, Crawley, Sussex.
Paperchase, Tottenham Court Road, London W1.

PAPER AND MATERIALS FOR DESIGN
Winsor and Newton Ltd, 51 Rathbone Place, London W1.
Reeves and Sons Ltd, Lincoln Road, Enfield, Middlesex.
George Rowney and Co. Ltd, 10 Percy Street, London W1.

CARDBOARD AND MILLBOARD
Artists' suppliers, printing firms, educational suppliers.

HARDBOARD AND WOOD
Local timber merchants or Do-it-Yourself shops.

ADHESIVES
Flameless rubber solution, from millinery trade suppliers.
Marvin Medium, Margros Ltd, Woking, Surrey.
Evo-stik and Copydex, from stationers and Do-it-Yourself shops.

Suppliers (America)

FABRICS
Garment Local sewing center, fabric shops, and most department stores.
Decorator Upholstery fabric shops, home-furnishing suppliers, most department stores.
Theatrical Danzian's, Inc., 40 East 29th Street, New York, N.Y.

TRIMMINGS AND ACCESSORIES (embroidery supplies, fringes, braid, cords, threads, silks, beads, feathers, etc.)
Drapery, dress and knitgoods trimming shops, millinery suppliers, notions, novelties, and handicraft shops, the notions counter in department stores. For a complete handicraft supplies mail-order catalogue, write to: American Handicrafts Co., Inc., 20 West 14th Street, New York, N.Y.

LEATHER
Local leather suppliers.

COLOURED ACETATE, CARDBOARD, ILLUSTRATION BOARD, AND ART SUPPLIES
Local art supplies stores. For a complete art supplies mail-order catalogue, write to: Arther Brown & Bro., Inc., 2 West 46th Street, New York, N.Y. or A. I. Friedman, Inc., 25 West 45th Street, New York, N.Y.

HARDBOARD
Lumberyard or building suppliers.

ADHESIVES AND STRING
Hardware, paint or art supplies store.

Index